Other 'crazy' gigglebooks by Bill Stott
Sex – it drives us crazy!
Marriage – it drives us crazy!
Rugby – it drives us crazy!
Cats – they drive us crazy!

Published simultaneously in 2004 by Helen Exley Giftbooks in Great Britain, and Helen Exley Giftbooks LLC in the USA

12 11 10 9 8 7

Selection and arrangement copyright © 2004 Helen Exley
Cartoons copyright © 2004 Bill Stott
Design by <rog@monkeyboydesign.co.uk>

ISBN 978-1-86187-755-0

A copy of the CIP data is available from the British Library on request.

Printed in China

Helen Exley Giftbooks, 16 Chalk Hill, Watford, Herts, WD19 4BG, UK
www.helenexleygiftbooks.com

A HELEN EXLEY
GIGGLEBOOK

Football

T DRIVES US CRAZY!

ARTOONS BY BILL STOTT

"Come on lads. I'm keeping it simple this week..."

"Your million dollar bargain just tied his own bootlaces together."

"Why are we out of the Cup? Well, I think it's because our team's useless and we've scored ONCE in nineteen matches..."

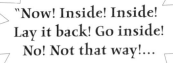

"And from here I can see that Rover's No. 7 isn't happy with that decision..."

"O.K. I want a nice open pattern – Dean and Ga
making runs down the flanks, Tommo and
Wayne drawing in their defenders. While al
this is going on, you Eric, will run about
kicking anybody you don't recognize..."

"...ook! A sponsor's a sponsor – now put it on!"

"Our Gary's soccer crazy – he's out in the yard trying out his dives..."

"...'s that new signing Boss – the chaps are just making sure he knows how to roll about and scream in agony at the slightest contact with an opposing player..."

"False eyelashes may be a first in the world of football face painting, but I'm not sure I wa to sit with you..."

"Timbuktu v Outer Mongolia... Oh goody!"

"He's going through his after-goal
crowd adulation response..."

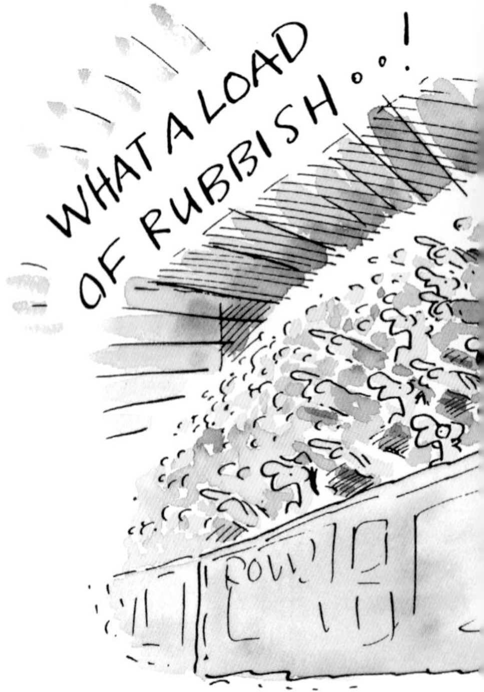
WHAT A LOAD
OF RUBBISH...!

"Relax, providing there's no extra time,
we'll make the church, easy!"

"Smile...!"

"His dad's very worried about him – he wants a referee's outfit for Christmas!"

"Then Grandad said 'Here's one I bet they
don't teach you at school' and kicked it
straight through the new window..."

"Well Brian, at the end of the day, the ref's decision is final, despite him being a two-face lying rat who's probably on the take."

Don't tell me. Shanghai v Manila... right?"

"I hate it when the referee is fair and you **still** get beaten..."

"My Youth Club is organizing a 'Dads' and 'Kids' match. Please, please come and...

". be an assistant referee?"

"Look at that. Not a blink.
    And he knows the score at the end!"

"Isn't that Saturday's ref?"

They always do that – the only other time
they line up together is to face a free kick..."

"Huh – seven nil. We don't support
our team. We prop them up!"

1

"Great goal, Gary. Gary? …Where's Gary?"

"I said, 'My mother's coming to stay for a month. The kids have run away and your car's on fire!'"

"Well, we've had a pretty lively debate
here tonight..."

here's a guy in the dugout wants a word
ith you. He's a Hollywood talent scout..."

don't suppose there's anything in the ules about that, Ref?"

"Huh! They've even got better names than u

"Their No. 7 was good, wasn't he?"

About Bill Stott

Bill Stott is a freelance cartoonist whose work never fails to pinpoint the absurd and simply daft moments in our daily lives. Originally Head of Arts faculty at a city high school, B launched himself as a freelance cartoonist in 1976. With sale of 2.8 million books with Helen Exley Giftbooks, Bill has an impressive portfolio of 26 published titles, including his ver successful *Spread of Over 40's Jokes* and *Triumph of Over 50's Jokes*

Bill's work appears in many publications and magazines, ranging from the *The Times Educational Supplement* to *Practical Poultry*. An acclaimed after-dinner speaker, Bill subjects his audience to a generous helping of his wit and wisdom, illustrated with cartoons drawn deftly on the spot!

hat is a Helen Exley giftbook?

hope you enjoy *Football – it drives us crazy!*. It's just one of many
rious cartoon books available from Helen Exley Giftbooks,
f which make special gifts. We try our best to bring you the
niest jokes because we want every book we publish to be
t to give, great to receive.

EN EXLEY GIFTBOOKS creates gifts for all special occasions
ot just birthdays, anniversaries, weddings and Christmas, but
hose times when you just want to say 'thanks' or 'I love you'.
y not visit our website, www. helenexleygiftbooks.com, and
vse through all our present ideas?

O BY BILL STOTT

rriage – it drives us crazy!
s – they drive us crazy!
gby – it drives us crazy!
– it drives us crazy!

mation on all our titles is also available from
n Exley Giftbooks, 16 Chalk Hill, Watford WD19 4BG, UK. Tel 01923 250505